Staying Out Late,
Playing Out Late

The poems in this book are
dedicated to Stewart and Carol.
For inspiration, encouragement
and friendship. Thank you.

Staying Out Late, Playing Out Late

and other poems

Paul Cookson
Illustrated by Nigel Baines

LION
Children's Books

Text copyright © 2003 Paul Cookson
Illustrations copyright © 2003 Nigel Baines
This edition copyright © 2003 Lion Publishing

The moral rights of the author and illustrator
have been asserted

Published by
Lion Publishing plc
Mayfield House, 256 Banbury Road,
Oxford OX2 7DH, England
www.lion-publishing.co.uk
ISBN 0 7459 4812 X

First edition 2003
1 3 5 7 9 10 8 6 4 2 0

A catalogue record for this book is available
from the British Library

Typeset in 12/16 Century ITC Book BT
Printed and bound in Great Britain
by Cox & Wyman Ltd, Reading

Contents

Prayer for the First Day of the School Holidays

Dear God... please...

Let rain be banished and the sun be strong
Let time pass slowly and the days be long

Let laughter echo forever with friends
Let fun and games be without end

May good days be many and bad days be few
May parents not find odd jobs for you

May bikes be indestructible and balls not be lost
May day trips be bountiful whatever the cost

May school be something we never remember
Let it always be August and never September

Thanks
Amen

Staying Out Late, Playing Out Late

Staying out late, playing out late
Staying out, playing out late with mates
Staying out late, playing out late
Staying out, playing out late is great

Football, tig, hide and seek
Swings and slides and roundabouts
Water fights and mountain bikes
We like staying, playing out...

Staying out late...

Making dens, hanging round
Songs to sing and jokes to shout
Rope swings and silly things
We like staying, playing out...

Staying out late...

Staying out – all day long
Playing out – late at night
We like staying, playing out
Everything's all right

Staying out late, playing out late
Staying out, playing out late with mates
Staying out late, playing out late
Staying out, playing out late is great!

No Better Feeling

There's no better feeling in the world
than the first morning of the holidays...
no rush... no panic...
no hassle... no worries...

the hours and days stretch ahead,
blank pages to be filled,
adventures to colour in,
memories to write,
excitement to record.

There's no better feeling in the world
than the first morning of the holidays...
lying in bed, staring at the ceiling
or just daydreaming out of the window...

daydreaming of how to fill those empty pages
and how you will enjoy each moment perfectly.

And those moments start right now...
in bed...
no rush...
no panic...
no hassle...
no worries...

Nothing

No school
No lessons
No test
No revision
No homework
Nothing to do in the holidays
Right then
What shall we do first?
No ideas?
Nothing to do in the holidays.

Just Jacko

Jimmy likes Joanne
but Joanne likes Jonathan
who only has eyes for Jane.
Jane likes Joe
but Joe likes Julie.
Julie doesn't know this
and thinks he likes Jenny
so she likes Jeffrey instead.
Jenny likes Jeffrey as well
but Jeffrey likes Judy.
Judy ignores him as she likes John
but John likes Janet
who in turn likes Jimmy.

Jacko couldn't care less.
He likes football and chocolate best.

Left Out

I'd never really spoken to him before.
Didn't really know him –
seen him with the others,
he was always there or thereabouts.

Always tagging along,
I thought he was a bit weird,
trying to join in their conversations
but always getting laughed at.

I'd laughed at him too,
from a distance.
Didn't really know him –
never really spoken to him before.

Until today.
We were both left out.
Started talking, got on okay,
turns out he thought the same about me.

Made a new friend today.
Think he'll be a good friend too.
Wish we'd spoken before.
So does he.

Dad Said

Dad said
he could beat us
blindfolded
with one leg tied behind his back.

He was wrong.

We ran rings round him
and beat him.

10–9
after extra time.

New Striker

Our team has got a brand new striker...
Sergei Callifragilistickexpialidocious.

I like him so much
Dad bought me a shirt with his name on the back.
And on the front.
And down both arms.

And on the shorts as well.

Secret

We've got a den,
it's brilliant, the best den in the whole wide world
but I can't tell you where it is –
it's secret.
Top secret.

We meet there every day,
except when it rains
because it floods near the brook,
but I can't tell you where it is –
it's secret.
Top secret.

When I say we,
I mean our gang,
just the four of us – the Fearless Four.
Sometimes there're five of us when Woody comes
(and he's only small so it's the Fearless Four
    and a Half)
but I can't tell you who is actually in our gang –
it's secret.
Top secret
(apart from Woody… and me…)

There's a special password.
Without it you can't come in our den,
except for Suzi who keeps forgetting it
and anyway she can't say
Spottybottylemonmeringuecurlywurlycowpat
but I can't tell you our password –
it's secret.
Top secret.
Nearly…

In our secret den we keep our special things
like comics, cards, sweets and cans of pop
and other things our parents don't know about –
especially Sunil and Tyrone's.
Boy will they be mad when they find out
what we've done with the lawnmower and
    that pram
but I can't tell you what –
it's secret.
Top secret.
Most of the time...

We play secret games in our den
and have important discussions
about the tricks we'll play on you know who
(except you don't know who – it's a secret)
and other important things we're going to do
but I can't tell you –
they're secret as well.
And important.

Yeah, we've got a den,
it's brilliant, the best den in the world
and it's ours.

Our secret.

All the Girls

All the girls gang up on Jane
Just because she's not the same
Her trainers are too cheap and plain
So... all the girls gang up on Jane.

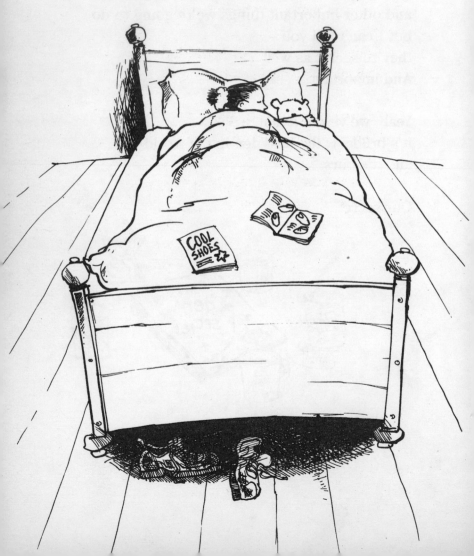

Never

I never saw his smile
I always saw the glasses and hearing aid

I never saw her sparkling eyes
I always saw the wheelchair

I never heard his words of kindness
I always heard the cleft lip

I never heard her laugh
I always heard the stammer

I never saw and never heard
I never got too close.

The Girl on the News

Was my age,
liked the same music,
even had the same trainers.

Had a David Beckham shirt,
watched Coronation Street
and did Irish dancing.

Loved books by J.K. Rowling
and Jacqueline Wilson, had the full sets,
just like me.

For dinner she'd had a chicken sandwich,
crisps and a Mars bar ice cream.
I love them, they're my favourites too.

She loved the park... so do I,
in fact that was the last place anyone saw her
before she was...

If she'd have been at my school
we could have been friends,
best friends... definitely best friends.

But she won't now, missing for ten days
and even though nobody's said so we sort of know
there's not going to be a happy ending.

She was my age, just like me.
It could have been me that was taken.
I could have been the girl on the news.

She had the same colour eyes
and I was going to do my hair like that,
exactly like that...

But I don't think I will now,
I don't think I will now,
I don't think I will now.

It Just Is

When you know in your heart
what's right is right,
it just is,
and nothing can make it wrong.

Teasing and taunting and unkind words
can make it hard, really hard,
but they can't make
what you know in your heart is right
wrong.

Sometimes it would be easier
not to believe the things you believe to be right,
because then you wouldn't feel guilty
about doing nothing.

But when you know it's wrong
to hate and hurt and lie and cheat
how can you pretend it's okay
and do nothing about it?

Why Parents Are Bonkers

Wide awake, late at night,
I'm playing out and it's still light –
What do Mum and Dad do?
They make me go to bed!

In the morning, fast asleep,
Comatose and in a heap –
What do Mum and Dad do?
They get me up instead!

When Mum Gets Really Mad
She Says...

You drive me crazy, up the wall
Round the bend you drive me mad
I've had it up to here with you
I've had enough of you my lad...

You drive me bonkers, barmy
You're going to drive me potty
You'll drive me to distraction
You're going to drive me dotty

You really make my blood boil
You'd swear that white is black
You'd drive a saint to swearing
You're the last straw on the camel's back

You do my head in, stress me out
You're a pain in the neck and a pain in the gut
You get on my nerves and up my nose
You're a pain in the rear and a pain in the... foot

You make me pull my hair out
You really make me sick
You rub me up the wrong way
You wind me up, get on my wick

You go on and on and on
You don't know when to stop
You'd better get out of my sight
Before I BLOW… MY…
TO…O…O…P…PPPP!!!!

Raining

It's raining, it's pouring
Holidays are boring
It's pouring, it's raining
I hate staying in

It's bucketing and sheeting
Nobody is meeting
It's throwing down and chucking down
We're not allowed to muck around

The rain is never ending
Mum won't allow a friend in
It's raining, it's pouring
Wet days are...

I Did Not Paint the Goldfish Blue

I may have broken Mum's best vase
And flushed the flowers down the loo
I may have eaten all the cake
And bent my brother's roller skates
I'll tell you this and no mistake...
I did not paint the goldfish blue

I may have smeared the toilet seat
With cold custard and superglue
I may have ruined dad's career
With maggots in his boss's ear
But let me say it loud and clear...
I did not paint the goldfish blue

I may have sneezed upon the veg
That Mum mixed in her Irish stew
I may have burped on Cousin Ruth
And left the hamster on the roof
There's no proof but it's the truth…
I did not paint the goldfish blue

I did not shave next door's cat
Or open cages at the zoo
I did not have the toothpaste blacked
Or know that Grandma's glass was cracked
I'll tell you this and it's a fact…
I did not paint the goldfish blue

We..e..ll

I may have used some purple paint
With some green, like you do...
I may have added black and grey
And some red, by the way
But I'm not telling lies when I say...
I did not paint the goldfish blue

I painted it purple, green, black, grey and red
Instead.

Just Mum and Me

We didn't do anything special today,
just Mum and me.
Raining outside, nowhere to go,
just Mum and me.

So we baked and talked and talked and baked
and baked and talked,
just Mum and me.

She told me about when she was young
and how her gran baked exactly the same cakes
on rainy days and baked and talked to her.

She remembered her friends
and the games they used to play,
the trees they used to climb,
the blackberries they picked,
the fields they used to run around in
and how summers always seemed to be sunny.

And Mum smiled a smile I don't often see,
the years falling away from her face,
and just for a moment
I caught a glimpse of the girl she used to be.

We didn't do anything special today,
raining outside, nowhere to go,
so we baked and talked and talked and baked,
just Mum and me.

I ate and listened and listened and ate,
the hours racing by so quickly.

We didn't do anything special...
but it was special, really special.

Just Mum and me.

I Want to Be Bad

Darth Vader is my hero
I wish he was my dad
I just want to dress in black
I want to be bad

I pull the legs off spiders
And disembowel flies
I like to drop live earwigs
On my sleeping sister's eyes
I'm good at stretching slugs
I bite the shells off snails
Then put them on my sister's head
With all their sticky trails

Darth Vader is my hero
I wish he was my dad
I just want to dress in black
I want to be bad

I colour all her colouring books
With deepest darkest black
Wipe bogies on the pages
Before I put them back
I twist the arms off baby dolls
And snap off Teddy's head
Then cover it with ketchup
And leave it in her bed

Darth Vader is my hero
I wish he was my dad
I just want to dress in black
I want to be bad

I'm evil and I'm nasty
The best at being worst
If badness was a race
Then I would be the first
I fear nothing, no one
I'm master of my doom
But when my sister tells my mum...
I'm banished to my room.

Stuck on Level One

Dad's on level six, so is my mum.
Me – I'm stuck, stuck on level one.

Brother's level seven, sister's level three.
Everybody's doing well... except me.

Stuck on level one is not much fun.
I hate going on when I'm stuck on level one.

I never find the clues, I cannot fire the gun,
Always slow, so... stuck on level one.

I forget which button makes me run,
Forever getting lost, stuck on level one.

I can't shoot straight and my power is gone,
I hate being rubbish, stuck on level one.

Dad's on level six, so is my mum.
But me – I'm stuck, stuck on level one.

Brother's level seven, sister's level three.
Everybody's doing well... except me!

Love Poem For...

I just can't wait to be with you
Time flies by when you are there
You take me to another place
Just me and you and a comfy chair

You fill my head with images
And feelings I can't wait to share
You touch all my emotions
Just me and you and a comfy chair

Where you go I follow
You can take me anywhere
Horizons disappear with you...
A favourite book and a comfy chair.

Wildest Dreams

In our wildest dreams
We...

Save the world from evil in a superhero style,
Score the winning World Cup Goal,
Sing Number One hit after hit,
Receive Oscars for our blockbuster movies,
Hit the winning six in a Test Match,
Win Wimbledon with ease and style
And write a story so brilliant it outsells Harry Potter.

In our wildest dreams
We do all these and more.

And still get home in time for tea.

The Magic Kitchen Carpet

There's a magic kitchen carpet
On the kitchen floor,
Weather-beaten, moth-eaten,
Just behind the door.

Food-stained, colour-drained,
It's shabby and it's torn.
Dead-bare, thread-bare,
Weathered and it's worn.

On this tattered magic carpet
You can choose your destination.
Any wild adventure,
Any situation.

When the cooking's bubbling
We're somewhere hot and tropical.
When wearing Grandma's glasses
We're somewhere microscopical.

When the ironing is steaming
We're deep in the Sahara.
Red Indians on the warpath
When wearing Mum's mascara.

When the washer overflows
We're in shark-infested seas.
When the freezer door is open
We are in an Arctic breeze.

We are rockets high in space
When Mum does the hoovering.
When she's moving chairs and tables
We are war planes out manoeuvring.

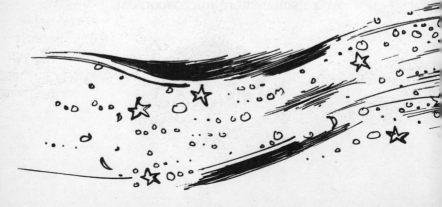

Assorted jars and bottles mean
Experiments and science.
When Dad leaves his wellies out
We're in the land of giants.

There's a magic kitchen carpet
Just behind the door,
Weather-beaten, moth-eaten,
Covering the floor.

On this tattered magic carpet
You can choose your destination
Because nothing's quite as magical
As your imagination.

Big Brothers' Jokes

Big brothers know the rudest jokes
They're wicked and they're bad
But don't repeat big brothers' jokes
In front of Mum and Dad!

Fishing with Uncle John

The two of us, five o'clock in the morning
and the sunrise pulling back
the misty water's blanket.

Not a sound, save the whirr of reels,
the swish of lines and the plop of bait,
not that we caught anything.

Eventually, the bird song
and hum of bugs invisible,
the occasional mini chainsaw buzz of bees
or the gloating splash of free fish.

The roll of Uncle's eyes at our failure,
the crazy smile of 'Why are we here?!'
and the fish and chips in the car on the way home.

The Day the Rope Swing Broke

I'm glad that it was not my go
High and low and to and fro
Above the water down below
The day the rope swing broke

I'm glad that I was high and dry
I'd be a liar to deny
I laughed enough to make me cry
The day the rope swing broke

I'm so glad he was the one
Much too heavy to get on
A moment later he was gone
The day the rope swing broke

A rush of air and then a splatter
Feel the mud and water scatter
It serves Dad right for being fatter
The day the rope swing broke.

No One Scores When Nigel's in Nets

No one scores when Nigel's in nets.
He's only four foot six,
thin as a straw,
glasses like jam jar bottoms,
hair over his eyes,
muscles like knots in cotton
and legs like broken matchsticks.

Still, no one scores when Nigel's in nets.
He brings his wolfhound,
Dogzilla,
who sits menacingly by the goalposts,
foaming at the mouth,
slobbering tongue
slowly licking gigantic green fangs,
howling that bloodcurling howl
and hungrily watching the game
through crimson crazed eyes.

Yes, no one scores when Nigel's in nets.
In fact no one comes into the penalty area.
Not even his own team.

Crick—ed

The bowler bowled a vicious ball
That caught me something wicked
It bounced and rose and smashed my nose
So dow I dust hade crick-ed.

Skateboard Surprise (A Tanka)

Dad fell off at once
Sister lasted down the path
I thought I was the best
Till Mum went round the block twice
Balancing on her hands.

Suffering in Silence

Mum shouted... but my sister just stood there.
Dad shouted... and she never said a word.
They both shouted angrily... and she stayed silent.

They grounded her, sent her upstairs
and all the time she just kept quiet,
never told them the awful truth
that I was the one who broke the window.

I never said anything either.
I should have done, I know that now.
I should have told the truth
but I didn't.

She took the blame
and I let her.
I owe her, big time.
Saying thank you's not enough...

but it's a start.

The Downhill Racers

Pushing pedals, setting paces
Windblown hair and smiling faces
Grinning, winning, speeding aces
We're the downhill racers

Great adventures, going places
Rocket ships to lunar bases
Motorcycle cops on chases
We're the downhill racers

Thrills and spills – faster, faster!
Gliding wheels sliding past you
Hear the squeals and shouts of laughter
We're the downhill racers

Hi-octane adrenaline pumping
Hammer pounding, heartbeat thumping
Wild excited jumping, bumping
We're the downhill racers

Wheels of fire – we're fanatics
On cloud nine – we're ecstatic
Mad for it – we're cyclopathic
We're the downhill racers

The urge to surge downhill's appealing
Nothing else can beat this feeling
Leading, speeding and freewheeling
We're the downhill
                downhill
                      racers!

Bubbles and Gum

Ben blows bubblegum bubbles best
He coolly slowly blows then stops
Ben blows the biggest gum bubble bubbles
Ben's bubblegum bubbles never pop

I blew a bubble a bit like Ben's
I thought that it was cool and ace
But I couldn't stop so it burst and popped
And gummed up all my hair and face.

Hide and Seek

One, two, miss a few... ninety-nine, a hundred.
Ready or not here I come!

I never liked being on.
Hiding's always much more fun
but why is it
that when you find the best hiding place ever
you always want to go to the toilet
before you've been found
and you have to decide whether to move and go
or stay still and squeeze
(just in case you do move and go)...

I can see you... come on out!

I can't really
but if you pretend you can
someone always does come out
and you've fooled them.
You've just got to sound confident.

In that bush there, I saw it move...

I know you're there,
I was peeping through my hands
while I was counting.

But there's always someone who can't be found
who thinks they're really clever
because they've managed to
disguise themselves as a tree, or a bird's nest,
hidden in a kennel or disguised themselves
    as a cowpat.

Well... I can't be bothered,
I leave them.
Pretend that I'm still playing
but go home for my tea.

They'll come out... eventually.

Staying Out Too Late

Sorry I'm late,
Didn't realize what time it was,
We were having such a great laugh.

No, I didn't think you'd be worried,
I was only round the corner,
You knew I was at Tom's.

Yes, I forgot my watch,
Yes, I can tell the time,
Yes, Tom's mum does have a clock,
Yes, I could have asked her.

I didn't think it was that late,
Well, time flies when you're having fun,
That's what you always say isn't it?
Well, time flies when you're having fun,
I didn't think it was that late.

Ye-es, I could have asked her,
Ye-es, Tom's mum does have a clock,
Ye-es, I can tell the time,
Ye-e-es, I forgot my watch.

You knew I was at Tom's,
I was only round the corner,
No-o-o-o... I didn't think you'd be worried.

We were having such a great laugh,
Didn't realize what time it was,
I'm late... sorry.

Doing Exactly as I Was Told

Do as you are told, they say,
Do exactly as you're told,
Do what I tell you.

Parents... they think they're so clever,
They think they know it all.
Do
      As
           You
               Are
                  Told!
Go and put your shoes and socks on.

So I do.
Exactly as I'm told.
First my shoes.
Then my socks.
Over the tops of my shoes so they stretch
And go wobbly at the front.

Mum comes in and goes ballistic...
*WHATDOYOUTHINKYOU'REDOINGMUCKING
ABOUTLIKETHAT?!*

I'm doing exactly as I'm told, Mum.
I'm putting my shoes... and my socks on.

DON'T BE SO STUPID!
USE YOUR COMMON SENSE!

Go and do your homework, she said.
Where? I said.
On the kitchen table, she said.
So I did.
Exactly as I was told.
Forty-seven sums and a story about my dog.
On the kitchen table.
No books or paper
Just... *on* the kitchen table.
In fact I did so much
I had to go down one leg as well.

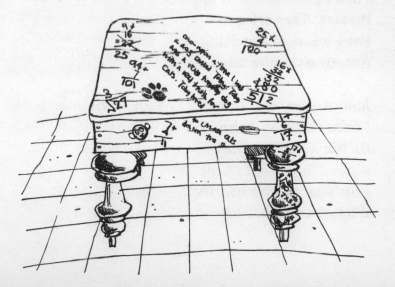

I'd just finished when Dad said,
Do us a favour... turn the telly over.
So I did.
Exactly as I was told.
I heaved and panted, pulled and pushed,
Grunted and groaned, nearly pulled a muscle,
Lifted and struggled until the screen was face
Down on the carpet.

I can't see the football!
What on earth are you doing?

I'm doing exactly as I was told.
I'm turning the telly *over.*

Then I got shouted at and sent to bed.
Parents! They tell you off,
Even when you're doing
Exactly as you're told.

And they say daft things... *Go and run your bath.*
Can't. Its got no legs.
Or *Put the kettle on.*
Why...? It doesn't fit me.
Can you put the cat out?
Why...? Is it on fire?

Come on hurry up, we're going to catch the bus.
I don't want to catch a bus, it'll break my arms.

So they say, *Don't be cheeky, watch your tongue.*
So you stick your tongue out and peer at it.
What are you doing now?
I'm doing exactly as I was told...
I'm watching my tongue.

Then they get really cross and start asking really
    stupid questions...
Do you want a smack?
Hmmmmmm... yes please, I'll have three, just to
    keep me going.
Do you want to go to bed without any tea?
What's for tea?
Broccoli and cabbage.
I'm going to bed now, thank you very much!

Innaminnit

Mum and Dad say...	Innaminnit
When I ask it's...	Innaminnit
Night and day it's...	Innaminnit
All the time it's...	Innaminniiiit!
Can I have...	Innaminnit
Can I go out...	Innaminnit
Can I watch...	Innaminnit
All the time it's...	Innaminniiiit!
Mum, look at this...	Innaminnit
Dad, can you help...	Innaminnit
Can you both come here...	Innaminnit
All the time it's...	Innaminniiiit!
But it's never...	Innaminnit
They don't know what's...	Innaminnit
I am sick of...	Innaminnit
It is always...	INNA–MINNIIIIIITTT!!!!

Actions Speak

He never said a word, my brother.
Just brought me a tissue – or two –
a cup of tea, chocolate biscuits
and his copy of *The Beano*.

Left them on my bedside table,
squeezed my shoulder, smiled
and left me alone for a while.

Never said a word.
Never had to.
Knew just how I felt.

Doing Exactly as I Was Told Again

On a ladder
… in the kitchen
… by the sink
… nearly touching the ceiling
… cleaning dirty plates above my head.

I was only doing as I was told.
Washing up.

Then I went down the ladder
… did the washing down
… stretched left and right – washing to the sides
   as well.

No Room to Swing a Cat

The caravan's full and that's a fact
Jammed and crammed and stacked and packed
Floor to ceiling, front to back
There's no room to swing a cat

Kitty's happy about that.

Together

On holiday it's different – there's a different side
   to Dad.
No phone, no letters, no work,
he just unwinds, lets it all hang out,
has the time to finish conversations,
the time to finish the newspaper and not just
   the sports page,
the time to laugh and joke,
the time to play our silly games,
the time to travel backwards and become a child
   with us.

The time to muck about,
splash water, kick footballs,
eat fish and chips, ice cream and pizza in the
   same afternoon,
the time to get told off by Mum
for being silly and setting us a bad example
(although she doesn't really mean it).

But best of all...
the time to be together.

A Brief Camping Holiday

When Dad forgot the camping stuff
We all found the campsite tough
One night and we'd had enough
We didn't stand a chance.

Everybody laughed at us
Stared and pointed, made a fuss
So embarrassing because
Dad made a tent with underpants
His massive spotty underpants
A makeshift tent of vast expanse
From purple spotted underpants
In the South of France.

blah blah blah blah blah blah blah......

Rambling with Dad

Dad loves rambling.
Rambles for ages and ages – on and on and on,
never stops, thinks we're keeping up with him,
just keeps going and going and going.

Once he starts, that's it.
Because he's interested he thinks we are too,
but we're not, we're bored
and we have to put up with it,
Dad rambling.

On and on and on.
And while he's walking
he's talking like he's walking...
rambling on and on and on
while he's rambling on and on and on.

Brother's Best at Sandcastles

Brother's best at sandcastles,
Loves the details and the plans,
Sticks and stones and shells are magic in his hands.

Like a sculptor sculpting,
A work of art displayed,
No hammer and no chisel, just a bucket and a spade.

Mine just crumble, mine just fall,
Ruins with no style at all.
His are full of moats and towers,
He works on them for hours and hours.

They may be something special
But even they cannot withstand
The ever creeping tide smoothing out the sand.

TERMINAL 4

Poetry
Postcards

Dear Jan,
We're fed up with all the delaying
we haven't arrived where we're staying
things aren't going well
and no one can tell
what the airport announcers
are saying.

Limerick

SKEGNESS

Dear David,
Skegness is okay
if you like sand and donkeys,
funfairs, fish and chips.

Haiku

POSTCARD

COS

Dear Gran,
Great time,
Sun burning hot,
The pool is fantastic,
Hotel's so good I don't want to
Come home.

Cinquain

Dear Roger
Dad sang like a cow in pain at the Karaoke
Mum and Gran fell over when they did the
Hokey Cokey

Brother got his hand stuck in the trouser press
Sister showed a bit too much when she split
her dress

I upset the manager – angry little fella
when I stained his shirt with a previous paella

This time next year we won't be here in Spain
we won't be invited back to this hotel again!

Couplets

A LOT

Why Do Fools Fall in... Love

I lost my heart at the swimming pool
The moment she walked by
My jaw dropped, I stared and stopped
Open-mouthed and goggle-eyed.

An angel in a swimsuit
A vision by the pool
Even in the sun she shone
Red hot and still ice cool.

She turned to meet my gaze and waved
Fluttering her eyes
And when she walked towards me
Imagine my surprise!

My legs turned to jelly
When she blew a kiss to me
My heart was pounding like a drum
Then missed a beat or three.

It skipped and flipped, I slipped and tripped
When she smiled again
I fell in love at the swimming pool
... and then I just fell in!

Swimming Pool Palindrome

Really embarrassing!
Whoops!
Oh no...
Dad dived in
As trunks came down
Whoosh! Splash! Aah! Splash! Splash!
Bottom bare!
Yikes!
Yikes!
Bare bottom!
Splash! Splash! Aah! Splash! Whoosh!
Down came trunks as
In dived Dad
No! Oh...
Whoops!
Embarrassing really!

Fairground Attraction

I knew she was the one for me
The moment I saw her.

My heart looped the loop
And helter-skeltered ever faster.

But I was like the coconut.
Shy.

Not a Good Idea

I had...
Candy floss, toffee apples, fizzy pop and hot dogs,
Popcorn, greasy chips, nougat bars and candy floss
Burgers, sugar dummies, sticks of rock and lollipops,
Ice cream, toffee apples, fizzy pop and candy floss

And then I went on the waltzers...
Up, down, round and round,
Round and round and round,
Left, right, side to side,
Round and round and round,
Stomach churning, ever turning,
Round and round and round and round,
Up, down, left, right,
Round and round and round...

I didn't half upset a lot of people.

Down to My Last Ten Pence

Down to my last ten pence
It's got to last all week
I won't be buying much at all
But I've got a bike and ball
And my friends will come and call
Bike rides, football, hide and seek
Things are not that bleak

Lack of funds won't stop me
Mucking round with mates
Loud music and stereos
TV, CDs, videos
Lots of places we can go
Things'll be just great
Staying out and playing late.

We are Busy Window Shoppin'
(A Rap)

We can look but we can't touch
We've no cash and we can't buy much
We can wish but we can't get
But – it's not stopped us yet
I said, but – it's not stopped us yet

We can live beyond our means
If we live within our dreams
We all love to fantasize
About our latest greatest buys
All our greatest buys

Hearts a pumpin', eyes a poppin'
We are busy **window shoppin'**
A hip hoppin' there's no stoppin'
We are busy **window shoppin'**

All the things that we would choose
The most expensive training shoes
Tons of chocolate, tons of sweets
Tons of things to drink and eat
Things to drink and eat

Skateboards, scooters, roller-boots
New computers and tracksuits
Mobile phones and DVDs
Ghetto blasters and CDs
Xbox and Playstation Two
Lots of things to play and do
Lots of things to play and do
Some for me and some for you
Look out 'cos we're comin' through

Hearts a pumpin' eyes a poppin'
We are busy **window shoppin'**
A hip hoppin' there's no stoppin'
We are busy **window shoppin'**

Though our pockets may be empty
We pretend that we have plenty
Re-tail thera-pee
Is even better when it's free
Even better when it's free

Hearts a pumpin' eyes a poppin'
We are busy **window shoppin'**
A hip hoppin' there's no stoppin'
Everybody **window shoppin'**

Fashion Statement

When I was younger
Mum would always buy clothes
at least three sizes too big
and I would say,
'Mum I can't go out in these,
they're too loose!'
to which Mum would reply,
'Don't worry, you'll grow into them.'

Now, when I wear my favourite jeans –
the ones that fray at the bottom –
and the hoody top,
Mum says,
'You can't go out in those,
they're far too loose!'
to which I reply,
'Don't worry, I'll grow into them.'

At the Cinema

When I go to the cinema
before the film starts
I like watching all the other people
watching the film
with their bins of popcorn
and buckets of fizzy pop.

They sit there transfixed,
hypnotized and goggle-eyed,
mechanically shovelling
handful after handful after handful
of popcorn into ever open mouths...

shovel chomp slurp
shovel chomp slurp
shovelchompslurpshovelchompslurpshovelchomp

But the best thing is when they come out after
like special effects
from the films they've been watching,
with bits stuck in their hair,
bits stuck on their jumpers
and bits stuck round their face...

INVASION OF THE POPCORN ALIENS!!!!!!!
SHOWING AT YOUR CINEMA RIGHT NOW!
BE CAREFUL... BE VERY VERY CAREFUL!

Happy Endings

All the family,
In the dark,
Watching a video,
Staying up late.

Home-made popcorn – gone.
Family bag of sweets – gone.
Two litres of Coke – gone.
Staying up late.

Sharing the jokes that we all laughed at,
The bumps and surprises that made us jump,
The bits that had us on the edge of our seats
    guessing,
And of course, the happy ending.

Just like us when the film is over.
Staying up late.
A happy ending.

On and On

If your mum says,
'Are you on the computer again?'
Just say, 'No,
I'm on the chair,
The computer's on the table.
If I was on it, then it would break
And then you'd tell me off.'

If your dad says, 'What's on the telly?'
Just say, 'A bowl of fruit and a photo.
They're on most tellies.'

The trouble is, I think in pictures,
Cartoons often.

I went into the kitchen.
Mum was there.
'Where's Dad?' I said.

'Oh... he's in the toilet.'
In... In the toilet.

Of course he wasn't in the toilet,
he was in the bathroom
but I still had that picture...

'Where's Grandad?'
'Oh... he's just popped out.'

Popped out!?
What's popped out?
Was his shirt too tight?

The Day We Built the Snowman

Round and round the garden,
Rolling up the snow,
One step, two step,
Watch the snowman grow.

Round and round the garden,
Us and Dad and Mum,
Building up the snowman,
Having lots of fun.

Mum has got a carrot,
Dad has got a pipe,
Sister's got a scarf
To keep him warm at night.

Baseball cap and shades,
Trainers for his feet,
Our trendy friendly snowman,
The coolest in the street.

Round and round the garden
In the winter weather,
The day we built the snowman...
Having fun together.

Prayer for the Last Day
of the School Holidays

Dear God
Thank you for the holidays, the sun and the shine
But if it's okay with you, can you please stop time?

May the school be closed and the staff be away
And please can we have just one more day?

And if you can't do these then please may it rain
So we don't feel bad about school time again

Thanks
Amen